CW01496276

Collection of Vietnamese Recipes

Cooking Vietnamese Foods at Home

Copyright © 2020

All rights reserved.

DEDICATION

Contents

Stir-Fried Sweet Shrimp

This simple Vietnamese shrimp recipe combines all the yummy flavors of the Southeast Asian part of the world into one package: The shrimp are salty, sweet, savory and spicy all at once. Plus, they are easy to stir-fry and take only a few minutes to cook.

Use decent-sized shrimp for this recipe (no smaller than 25 per pound) if you are serving this alone as an appetizer. If you want to top a rice dish with these shrimp to make the main course, you can use smaller ones.

Ingredients

1 pound unpeeled (uncooked shrimp)

1 tablespoon peanut or other vegetable oil

1 tablespoon sesame oil

1 1/2 tablespoons honey or light brown sugar

2 finely chopped garlic cloves

1 finely chopped shallot

1 to 3 finely chopped small hot chiles (such as Thai chiles)

4 tablespoons chicken or fish stock

1 tablespoon Asian fish sauce

1/4 teaspoon salt

2 tablespoon chopped cilantro

Steps to Make It

With a sharp knife, slice down the backs of the shrimp to expose the black "vein," which is the shrimp's digestive tract. Pull out this little vein, but keep the shells on the shrimp.

NOTE: These shrimp are served shell-on, which keeps them moister and gives them more flavor than if you removed the shell. But if shelling shrimp at the table is not for you, you can remove the shells and still make this dish.

A word on the chiles. You can adjust the heat any way you want. You could use 3 Thai chiles for some serious heat, or 1 full cayenne would be similar, as would half a habanero. Or you can use less to your taste—or none at all.

Heat the peanut oil and sesame oil in a saute pan over medium-high heat for a minute or two.

Add the shrimp and the honey or brown sugar and stir-fry for 1 to 2 minutes, then add the garlic and shallot and stir-fry for another minute or two.

Add the stock (you can use water if you do not have stock available), fish sauce and salt and turn the heat to its highest setting. Let this boil down until the pan is nearly dry, which should only take a minute or two.

Serve at once, garnished with the cilantro. This is excellent beer food, but a sweet-salty Thai limeade would be great, too (if you can't find Thai limeade, just add a pinch of salt to your favorite limeade brand). As for pairing with wine, go with a Gewurztraminer or an off-dry Riesling, or maybe a tropical-tasting Roussanne from California.

Lemongrass Tamarind Chicken

It is curious how one finds the basic sweet and sour dish in the cuisine of every Southeast Asian country. Filipinos have escabeche; the Thai have their pad preow wan wai (they even have a name for their sweet and sour sauce—nam jim priao wan); the Malaysians have a cooking style known as masak blandah/belanda, and there's this Vietnamese sweet and sour chicken dish with lemongrass and tamarind.

Unlike the basic Chinese sweet and sour sauce that is made by combining vinegar and sugar, the sweet and sour sauce of this chicken dish is made by mixing together sugar and tamarind juice. Yes, it is still sweet and sour but the tamarind gives the sauce a fruity and richer flavor that vinegar does not have.

There are three ways to get the tamarind juice you'll need to make this dish.

If you have access to fresh tamarind, rinse them and boil in just enough water to cover until mushy. Mash the softened tamarinds, strain and use the extracted juice.

Dried tamarinds sold in Asian stores must be soaked in hot water to soften. Discard the water, mash the tamarinds and use the extract.

The third and easiest method is to buy tamarind paste sold in jars in Asian stores. Note, however, that tamarind paste has sugar in it and is not as sour as tamarind juice. It is also darker. You may need to use a lot of tamarind paste to get the sourness you need and that means that the cooked dish will also be darker.

Ingredients

12 chicken thigh fillets, about 800 grams (cut into 1-1/2 inch cubes)

3 tablespoons fish sauce

2 heaping tablespoons brown sugar

2 red chili peppers (finely chopped)

2 green finger chilis (finely sliced)

4 cloves of garlic (minced)

Peppe (freshly ground)

2 stalks of lemongrass (white part only, finely sliced)

4 tablespoons vegetable cooking oil

3 to 4 tablespoons tamarind extract or paste, or to taste

1/2 cup chicken broth

1 carrot (thinly sliced) or one red bell pepper (cored and diced)

Garnish: Vietnamese cilantro(sometimes called Vietnamese mint) or cilantro (chopped)

Steps to Make It

In a bowl or resealable plastic bag, place the chicken, sugar, fish sauce, chilis, garlic, pepper, and lemongrass. Mix well and leave to marinate in the fridge for at least 30 minutes.

Heat the cooking oil in a wok or frying pan. Strain the chicken and lightly brown in the hot oil. Add the carrot slices (or diced bell pepper) and cook for another 30 seconds.

Pour in the marinade, broth and tamarind extract (or paste). Stir well. Lower the heat, cover and simmer for 10 minutes.

Transfer to a serving platter, sprinkle with cilantro and serve hot with rice.

Enjoy!

Cabbage Roll Soup

Depending on where you are in the world, cabbage rolls may be filled with meat, rice, chopped vegetables, mushrooms, and spices. The cabbage rolls may be steamed, baked or simmered and served with a sauce. The sauce can be sour cream, yogurt, tomato-based or made with lingonberry jam.

In Vietnam, cabbage rolls are served in broth. In most recipes, the meat-filled cabbage leaves are simmered in water until the rich flavors of the meat and the subtle sweetness of the cabbage permeate the cooking liquid. We prefer to use homemade broth instead of water.

Ingredients

1 head white cabbage

6 shallots (or 2 large red onions)

1 to 2 carrots

4 cloves garlic

400 grams ground pork (with at least 20 percent fat)

100 grams shrimp, shelled and minced

2 tablespoons cilantro, minced

2 teaspoons fish sauce, or to taste

1/2 teaspoon black pepper, or to taste

12 to 16 onion leaves

8 to 10 cups homemade broth

Steps to Make It

Gather the ingredients.

Prepare the cabbage by first removing the hard core. The core of the cabbage is shaped like a cone. If the cabbage is standing upright, the "mouth" of the "cone" is at the bottom. The opposite end of the cone ends about an inch or two below the top side of the cabbage. First, cut off the cone-shaped core. Position the cabbage with the base on top. Using a sharp, pointed knife held at a slight angle, cut into the core of the cabbage stopping about an inch or two from the opposite end. Rotating the cabbage little by little, repeat until you have cut around the base of the cire. If you did the procedure correctly, you should be able to pull out the entire core without much resistance.

Next, boil the cabbage until softened. Drop the cabbage into a pot with the hole pointing upward. Pour boiling water into the pot (I pour the boiling water directly into the hole) until the cabbage is completely submerged.

Place a heavy heatproof plate to keep the cabbage underwater.

Boil until softened. Depending on the size of the cabbage, this can take anywhere from 7 to 15 minutes.

Scoop out the cabbage, plunge in iced water and drain.

Separate the cabbage leaves taking care not to tear them. You need 12 to 16 whole cabbage leaves (you won't be able to use the small ones; keep them for another use). Using a small, sharp knife, cut off the thick white portion in the middle of each leaf. Start at the middle of each leaf and cut all the way down using as though paring a potato. The cabbage leaves are now ready to be used as wrappers.

Blanch the onion leaves in boiling water for a few seconds to wilt. Rinse well.

Peel and finely chop the shallots (or onions) and carrots.

Crush, peel, and finely mince the garlic.

Place the ground pork and minced shrimp in a bowl and add the chopped shallots, carrots, garlic, and cilantro. Season with fish sauce and ground pepper.

Lay a cabbage roll flat, the core end nearest you. Place 1 to 2 tablespoonfuls of filling at the center of the cabbage leaf.

Take the edge nearest you, fold over the filling.

Take the side edges and fold in.

Roll the whole thing outward to close and seal.

Take an onion leaf and use it to tie the cabbage roll. Repeat until all the cabbage leaves are stuffed and tied.

In a large cooking pot, bring the broth to a boil. Drop the cabbage rolls one by one. Wait until the broth is boiling once more then lower the heat, cover, and simmer for 10 to 15 minutes.

Serve hot and enjoy!

Lemongrass-Marinated Lamb Chops

Lemongrass has the amazing ability to tame the "gamy" flavor of lamb. In this Vietnamese recipe, lemongrass is finely chopped and combined with fish sauce and sweet mushroom sauce to give a robust flavor to the lamb chops. The chops need to marinate overnight, but then you can sear and bake them, as this recipe calls for, or pan-fry or barbecue them.

Ingredients

3 stalks fresh lemon grass

1 red hot chili pepper, chopped

1/2 teaspoon chopped garlic

1 teaspoon freshly cracked black pepper

1/2 teaspoon salt

3 teaspoons palm sugar

3 tablespoons fish sauce

1 teaspoon fresh lemon juice

1 tablespoon sweet mushroom soy sauce (or dark soy sauce)

4 large lamb chops, each 8 ounces or 8 small chops, each 4 ounces

2 cloves garlic, crushed

2 tablespoons brown sugar

2 tablespoons fresh lemon juice

2 tablespoons white wine vinegar

1 Thai bird's eye chili pepper, chopped

1 tablespoon canola oil

1/2 cucumber, diced

1 small tomato, diced

2 tablespoons chopped fresh cilantro

Steps to Make It

To make the marinade, cut each lemongrass stalk with a sharp knife about 3 to 4 inches from the bottom, where the light and green portions meet. Peel and discard the top layer of the light part of each stalk, revealing the tender, white inner hearts. Slice these and mince them finely. (Reserve the remaining green leaves to use in other dishes.)

In a medium bowl, combine minced lemon grass, chili peppers, garlic, black pepper, salt, sugar, fish sauce, lemon juice and soy sauce and stir until well mixed.

Place lemon grass marinade in a large shallow pan. Add lamb chops individually, spooning marinade all over the meat to ensure each chop is well coated. Cover with plastic wrap and refrigerate for 3 hours or up to 24 hours.

To make the dipping sauce, in a saucepan combine 1 cup water, garlic, and brown sugar and bring to a boil over medium-high heat. Reduce the heat to medium-low, constantly stirring for 1 minute until sugar melts, then turn off the heat.

Add lemon juice, vinegar, and chili peppers, stir well and transfer to a sauce bowl. (The dipping sauce will keep refrigerated in an airtight container for 3 to 4 weeks.)

About 30 minutes before cooking, remove lamb chops from the

refrigerator. Preheat the oven to 400 F.

Heat the canola oil in a large skillet over high heat. Let the marinade drip off the lamb chops, then add them to the skillet. Brown one side of the chops for 2 minutes. Turn lamb over and brown for another 2 minutes.

Transfer the skillet to the oven and bake for 5 to 10 minutes, or until cooked medium rare. Take the skillet out of the oven, and transfer the chops to a serving plate. Set aside.

Pour the marinade into a small saucepan and bring to a gentle boil on medium-high. Reduce the heat to low and simmer for 5 minutes. Pour the reduced marinade into a serving bowl.

Place cucumbers, tomatoes, and cilantro in individual serving bowls. Serve the lamb chops, family-style, with the marinade, dipping sauce, cucumbers, tomatoes and cilantro as condiments.

Stir-Fried Mixed Vegetables

Stir-fried vegetables are a versatile component in any Southeast Asian meal. They are a great accompaniment to grilled or fried meat or seafood. There are so many ways to cook them and the combination of vegetables is quite limitless. The Vietnamese rau xao distinguishes itself from the rest with the absence of heavy sauces like oyster sauce or kecap manis.

Add some meat or seafood to the vegetables and the dish becomes a complete meal when served with rice–easy to prepare and perfect for days when work takes a toll. If you are a vegetarian, omit the fish sauce and add some tofu instead of meat.

Ingredients

1/2 cup broccoli

1/2 cup cauliflower

1/2 cup green beans

1/2 cup baby corn

1/2 cup carrots

1/2 cup red peppers/capsicums

A few slices of zucchini

4 to 6 mushrooms (button or shiitake are recommended)

2 finely chopped cloves of garlic

2 tablespoons fish sauce

2 tablespoons oil

1 tablespoon rice wine

1/2 teaspoon white ground pepper

Salt to taste

Steps to Make It

Gather the ingredients.

In a pot or wok, bring 10 cups of water to a boil and add a teaspoon of salt.

Blanch the carrot, broccoli, and baby corn for 30 seconds.

Remove and soak these vegetables for ten seconds in cold water so that they do not get overcooked. Drain the vegetables.

Heat the oil in a wok or saucepan over low heat. Fry the garlic until golden brown.

Turn up the heat to high and add the blanched vegetables with the red peppers. Fry for 20 seconds and mix the vegetables well.

Add the rice wine, fish sauce, white pepper, and salt.

Stir well and serve the stir-fried mixed vegetables with plain boiled rice and any other Southeast Asian meat or seafood dish.

Enjoy!

Vietnamese Fried Rice

Fact: Every cuisine in Southeast Asia has been influenced by the Chinese in one or more ways.

Fact: Vietnamese cooking–with its sweet, spicy, salty, sour, and bitter flavors–is heavily influenced by the Wu Xing philosophy with each flavor corresponding with earth, metal, water, wood, and fire, respectively, or the Five Elements.

From those two facts alone, it is easy to glean how much Chinese cuisine has influenced Vietnamese cooking.

When it comes to fried rice, is there a difference between Chinese and Vietnamese fried rice? Yes, there is. Vietnamese fried rice has milder flavors because of its seasonings.

In this recipe, the sweetness of the lap cheong (dried fatty Chinese sausage) and the barbecued pork, and the saltiness of the fish sauce are balanced by a bit of lime juice.

Ingredients

2 tablespoons peanut oil

2 eggs (beaten with a drizzle of fish sauce)

1 stalk lemongrass (white portion only) (finely chopped)

2 cloves garlic (minced)

2 shallots (finely chopped)

1/4 cup carrot (chopped)

1/4 cup sweet peas (if using frozen, thaw completely)

1 lap cheong (thinly sliced)

1/2 cup barbecued pork (thin strips)

3 cups rice (cold cooked jasmine or other long-grain rice–not newly-cooked rice–rubbed to separate the grains)

Dash fish sauce (to taste)

1/2 tablespoon lime juice (juice of a quarter of lime)

1/2 cup cilantro (or lemon basil or mint, to garnish)

Steps to Make It

1. Heat the peanut oil in a wok or frying pan.
2. Pour in the beaten eggs. Cook, swirling often, just until set. Scoop out and transfer to a cutting board.
3. Over medium heat, saute the lemongrass, garlic, and shallots until softened and aromatic.
4. Turn up the heat, add the chopped carrot and sweet peas, and stir fry for half a minute.
5. Add the sliced lap cheong and the barbecued pork. Stir fry for about a minute.
6. Add the rice. Pour in about a teaspoonful of fish sauce. Stir fry until the rice is heated through. Turn off the heat.
7. Roll up the egg like a cigar and cut into thin slices. Add to the rice. Toss.
8. Squeeze the lime quarter over the fried rice. Toss a few more times.
9. Serve hot garnished with cilantro, lemon basil or mint, or all three.

Pork Chops

Take your go-to weeknight protein to the next level with these mouthwatering Vietnamese pork chops. They're full of salty, sweet, and tangy flavors, heightened by the uniquely fragrant profile of the lemongrass. Once you learn how to prep this simple herb, you'll want to use it all the time!

This recipe comes together quickly. You can serve the pork chops alongside warm white rice or flat rice noodles. You can also serve it with classic Vietnamese condiments like pickled carrots and nuoc cham, a tangy Vietnamese dipping sauce. Extra hoisin sauce is always welcome, and Sriracha doesn't hurt either!

Make Vietnamese Noodle Salad With Lemongrass Beef (Bun Bo Xao) at Home

Ingredients

4 pork chops (boneless, center-cut)

2 stalks lemongrass

2 tablespoons fish sauce

3 tablespoons hoisin sauce

1 teaspoon white vinegar

2 tablespoons sugar

1 teaspoon salt

1/2 teaspoon ground black pepper

1 clove garlic (minced)

1/4 cup oil for frying

Steps to Make It

Gather your ingredients.

Place pork chops in a shallow bowl or a plastic bag. Make sure either is large enough to fit the marinade as well.

Peel the outer coarse layers of the lemongrass away. After removing the root, finely chop the bottom third of each stalk.

Whisk together the fish sauce, hoisin sauce, vinegar, sugar, salt, black pepper, and minced garlic with the lemongrass. Whisk in a tablespoon of water as well.

Pour the marinade over the pork chops. Cover with plastic wrap and allow them to marinate for thirty minutes in the refrigerator.

Heat up the oil in your skillet to a medium-high heat. Add the pork chops in a single layer. If they don't fit in a single layer, fry them in batches.

Fry on one side until browned, about four minutes. Flip and continue frying on the second side until browned and cooked through. Add the rest of the marinade to the pan and allow it to reduce and thicken slightly.

Serve the pork chops immediately on top of rice or rice noodles with a sprinkle of scallions or chives.

Tips

Whisk in a tablespoon of cornstarch to the marinade before adding it back to the pan to thicken. This will create a thicker, glossier sauce.

Variations

You can grill these pork chops instead of pan-frying them. You can thicken the marinade in a separate pan on the stovetop or grill or just don't add the extra marinade at the end. They will be delicious either way.

The flavor from the grill adds a great dimension to the pork chops and is the perfect choice for the summer months when it's too hot to cook inside!

You can marinate the pork chops for up to four hours before cooking. Too much longer and the meat will start to "cure" in the acidic vinegar.

Instant Pot Pho

Pho is Vietnam's national dish and just one spoonful will tell you why.

A wonderfully fragrant, subtly spiced broth is the secret to a delicious bowl of pho and an Instant Pot will help you become a true master of the noodle soup. The broth can take as long as six hours on the stovetop, but it takes requires 40 minutes in the Instant Pot. The cooking time is relatively short, but make sure you allow plenty of time—about an hour—for pressure to build up and release naturally.

Any electric or stovetop pressure cooker may be used, but make sure to adapt as needed to follow the manufacturer's recommendations and safety precautions.

90 Delicious Recipes You Can Make in Your Instant Pot

Ingredients

For the Broth:

3 pounds beef shanks (soup bones)

1/2 pound beef chuck (stewing beef or brisket; 1 pound if the shanks are not very meaty)

2 whole star anise

1 (3-inch) cinnamon stick

1 teaspoon coriander seeds

2 whole cloves

1 large onion

1 1/2 ounces fresh ginger (about 2 1/2 inches)

8 cups water

1 tablespoon sugar

1 1/2 teaspoons kosher salt (or to taste)

1/2 teaspoon black pepper

1 tablespoon fish sauce (or to taste)

1 tablespoon soy sauce (or to taste)

For the Noodle Soup:

8 ounces rice noodles

10 to 12 ounces steak (sirloin, flank steak, top round)

3 cups bean sprouts

4 green onions (thinly sliced)

Steps to Make It

Note: While there are multiple steps to this recipe, the broth and soup are broken down into workable categories to help you better plan for preparation and cooking.

For the Broth

Gather the ingredients.

Place the beef shanks or soup bones and beef chuck in a 6-quart Instant Pot and cover with water. Choose the highest sauté function and bring the beef to a full boil. Continue to boil for five minutes. Carefully drain the beef and discard the liquids. Set the meat aside. Boiling and draining the beef ensures the final broth will be clear instead of cloudy.

Choose the normal sauté function and add the star anise, cinnamon stick, coriander seeds, and whole cloves. Cook, stirring frequently to prevent burning, for about five minutes, or until the spices are toasted and aromatic. Alternatively, toast the spices on the stovetop over medium heat, then add them to the Instant Pot.

Peel the onion and cut it in half lengthwise. Slice the halves thickly. Peel the ginger and cut it into small chunks. Add the onion slices and ginger to the pot along with two teaspoons of cooking oil and cook on the normal sauté setting until lightly charred, stirring frequently. Cancel the sauté function.

Add the drained beef and bones back to the pot along with eight cups of water. The level should be just under the max fill line of a six-quart pot. Add the sugar (if using), 1 1/2 teaspoons of kosher salt, and the pepper. Lock the lid in place and turn the steam release valve to "sealing." Select the manual setting, high pressure, and set the time to 40 minutes. When the time is up, let the pressure come down naturally for 20 to 25 minutes. Carefully turn the steam release valve to "venting" to release any remaining pressure.

Place the rinsed beef in the Instant Pot.

Using a slotted spoon, remove the meat, place in a bowl and set aside. Strain the liquids into a large bowl or pot through a fine mesh strainer, and discard the solids left in the strainer. Shred the beef and add it to the broth. Add one tablespoon each of fish sauce and soy sauce, then taste and adjust seasonings as needed. At this point, you may refrigerate the broth until you are ready to assemble and serve the soup.

Assemble the Soup

Bring the meaty broth to a simmer in a saucepan or in the Instant

Pot.

Cook or soak the rice noodles or rice sticks following the package directions; drain well. Slice the raw beef very thinly across the grain.

Add hot noodles to each bowl, followed by several strips of raw beef. Spoon some of the red and green onions over the beef, then ladle hot broth over all. Finish with 1/2 to 3/4 cup of bean sprouts, cilantro, sliced chili pepper, and other garnishes, as desired.

Enjoy your beef pho!

Tips

If you would like to cut back on the fat content, refrigerate the broth until the fat solidifies. The fat provides richness and flavor, so leave at least a few tablespoons.

If you aren't sure you'll like the flavor of fish sauce, add it in small amounts along with the soy sauce, tasting as you go.

The hot broth will cook the thinly sliced beef, but if you prefer well-done meat, broil or pan grill the steak before slicing, or briefly stir-fry the slices.

Pho Bo Soup

Today there is no dish that is more associated with Vietnamese cuisine than phở, even though the dish's 120-year-old history is a mere blip in the timeline of Vietnam's 4,900-year civilization. Its exact origins are still uncertain but everyone agrees it originated from the north, in or near Hanoi, as an evolution of xáo trâu, a noodle soup made with water buffalo meat. Due to French colonization around the 1900s, the demand for beef grew as French officials wanted dishes from back home (at that time in Vietnam, cows were seen only as draft animals, the way we see horses today). The bones and unwanted scraps from the French beef were purchased by xáo trâu vendors and used in place of water buffalo, and thus phở was born.

After the Geneva Agreement of 1954 which created two Vietnams: a north and south, almost a million northerners migrated south, bringing phở along with them. Because the southerners have more of a sweet tooth and an abundance of herbs, they added rock sugar, coriander and fennel seeds to the broth; they served the meal with an abundance of Thai basil, culantro, beansprouts, hoisin and chili sauce (all marked as optional below). The dish was once again transformed.

And in 1975 when the north reunited itself with the south, there was a large exodus of southern Vietnamese. Many of them settled in the U.S., France, Australia, etc. and opened up their own restaurants serving southern-style phở.

Knowing the history of phở takes away much of the intimidation and pressure to make the dish "authentically." It's a relatively modern dish that in its short history has already undergone massive transformation. The phở someone's mom makes will not taste like the phở someone else's mom makes because of upbringing, individual tastes, geographic availability of ingredients, etc. The most important thing is that phở comforts you, and if what you made does that, then you did it "right."

If the cook time is intimidating, know that most of it is inactive and all the prep can be done while waiting for the next step. So, see this as a chance to take a nap or binge a show.

Ingredients

For the Bones and Brisket:

6 pounds beef bone marrow

2 pounds brisket (or shank)

1/4 cup distilled white vinegar

1/4 cup salt

For the Broth:

2 gallons water

Optional: 1/2 cup rock sugar

3 tablespoons salt

2 (3-inch) pieces ginger

2 yellow onions

3 pieces whole star anise

10 whole cloves

1 black cardamom pod

1 cinnamon stick

Optional: 3 teaspoons coriander seeds

Optional: 2 teaspoon fennel seeds

1/2 cup fish sauce

For the Bowls:

2 (14-ounce or 16-ounce package) pho noodles (prepared according to package direction)

1 pound filet mignon (sliced thinly against the grain)

1 red onion (sliced thinly into half rings and stored in cold water)

4 green onions (white parts thinly sliced lengthwise, green parts chopped in a circular cut)

Optional: 1 bunch cilantro leaves (roughly chopped)

For Serving (all optional):

8 sprigs Thai basil

8 culantro leaves

2 cup bean sprouts (blanched)

4 Thai bird's eye chilies (with seeds, finely sliced)

2 limes (quartered lengthwise into slices)

Hoisin sauce

Chili sauce (such as sriracha)

Steps to Make It

Note: while there are multiple steps to this recipe, this recipe is broken down into workable categories to help you better plan for preparation and cooking.

Prepare the Bones and Brisket

Gather the ingredients for the bones and brisket.

Place the bones and brisket in a large stock pot. Fill the pot with enough cool water to cover the bones and add the salt and vinegar. The acidity of the vinegar starts the process of drawing nutrients from the bones before you even start cooking. Soak for 1 to 2 hours. Drain and rinse the meat and bones of the salt and vinegar. Return the bones and brisket to the pot.

Pour enough water to cover the bones and brisket again. Bring to a boil and cook at a rapid simmer for 10 minutes. At this point, a lot of foam and impurities should have risen to the top (if not, cook for another 5 to 10 minutes until it does). Drain, rinse the bones and brisket, and return them to the pot. Similar to the previous step, this is done to further remove impurities from the meat and bones to yield a clearer broth.

Make the Broth

Gather the ingredients for the broth.

Add 2 gallons of fresh, cool water, rock sugar, and salt to the stockpot with the bones and brisket and bring to a boil over high heat. Immediately, reduce the heat to a very low simmer and leave uncovered. In the beginning, a lot of foam and many impurities will float to the top; skim those out regularly.

Meanwhile, broil the ginger pieces and onions, so the skins starts to blacken. (Alternatively, cook over a gas flame until blackened.)

Rinse under running water to cool and peel the black skin off to release their fragrance. Add to the stockpot with the bones and brisket.

After the broth has cooked for 1 hour, check to see if the brisket is fully cooked through. If so, remove it from the stockpot and store it in cool water to keep it moist and prevent it from darkening.

After another hour has passed, heat a sauté pan over high heat. Toast the star anise, cloves, black cardamom, cinnamon stick, coriander seeds, and fennel seeds until just fragrant (1 to 2 minutes). Be careful not to burn them. Secure them in a sachet or tea bag and add them to the center of the stock pot. They may need to be weighed down by an onion or bone.

Simmer uncovered for 1 hour. At the broth has cooked for 3 hours total, season it with the fish sauce. Taste the broth and adjust seasoning, as necessary.

Simmer for another hour to let the new seasonings work their way into the broth. After 4 hours of broth making, once the taste is right, bring it up to a boil.

Assemble the Bowls

Gather the ingredients for the bowls.

Take the brisket out of its cool water storage and thinly slice against the grain.

Divide the prepared noodles among the four bowls, top with cooked brisket, raw filet mignon, red onion, green onion, and cilantro.

Ladle the boiling stock over each bowl, pouring over the raw meat first so it cooks right away. There should be enough stock to cover the beef in each bowl.

Serve

Gather the ingredients for serving.

Place Thai basil, culantro, beansprouts, and chili slices on a large serving plate for everyone to draw from and add to their bowls. Thai basil leaves should be plucked from their stems and torn in half to release their flavor.

Serve everyone a slice of lime to squeeze into their phở and a small bowl of hoisin and chili sauce to dip their meat in.

Pho should be eaten immediately after serving before the noodles get a chance to bloat up.

Sambal Kangkung With Shrimp Paste

Kangkung is Ipomoea aquatica, a semiaquatic plant that grows in swamps. It is called kangkong in Filipino, rau muống in Vietnamese, phak bung in Thai and kangkung in Malaysian and Indonesian. Both the hollow stalks and the leaves are edible although the stalks are tougher and take a bit longer to cook.

Sambal is a generic term for chili-based sauces; there are a lot of varieties, we suggest using sambal oelek (available in the Asian section of most groceries). If you use sambal belacan which is a chili and shrimp paste, you don't have to add shrimp paste separately, but you'll probably have to make adjustments to the amounts. You can serve this as a vegetable dish alongside a meat dish. It's not totally vegetarian because shrimp paste is an ingredient; if you want to transform it into a vegetarian dish, just omit the shrimp paste.

Ingredients

a large bunch of kangkong, rinsed

2 to 3 shallots, peeled and diced

6 cloves garlic, crushed and peeled

1 teaspoon finely minced lemongrass

2 tablespoons vegetable oil

1/2 teaspoon grated ginger

1 heaping tablespoon sambal oelek (or use 2 to 3 finely chopped bird's eye chilis)

1 teaspoon tamarind paste

1 teaspoon sugar

1/2 teaspoon shrimp paste fish sauce, to taste

Steps to Make It

Cut the kangkung into two-inch lengths. Separate into three portions—the thick lower stalks, the middle portion of the stalks and the leaves.

Grind the onion, garlic and lemongrass to a paste (a mortar and pestle are traditional, but you can also use a food processor).

Heat the cooking oil in a wok or frying pan. Add the onion-garlic-lemongrass paste, grated ginger, tamarind paste, shrimp paste, sugar, sambal oelek (or chilis, if that's what you're using) and about a teaspoonful of fish sauce. Cook gently over medium heat until the mixture separates from the oil.

Add the kangkung stalks—the thick ones. They take the longest to cook so they go into the pan first. Stir. Pour in about three tablespoonfuls of water and cook for about two minutes.

Add the middle portion of the stalks, stir, cook for a minute.

Add the kangkung leaves, stir and cook for about half a minute.

Taste, add more fish sauce if needed and serve hot.

Pomelo and Shrimp Salad

Pomelo is one of four non-hybrid citrus fruits. All other citrus fruits are hybrids derived from one or more of these four. Pomelo is a large fruit about six to ten inches in diameter and weighs anywhere from one to two kilograms. The edible pulp, however, is small relative to the size of the fruit. The bitter rind is thick and inedible.

Because of the size of the fruit, some fruit vendors make it convenient for buyers by selling the pomelo in segments. If an entire fruit is too much for you, buying a segment or two might be the smarter way to go. That way, you consume the pomelo before it dries out.

To use the pomelo pulp for making this salad, peel off and discard the skin that covers each segment of the fruit. Then use your hands to separate the pulp.

Shrimps go very well with pomelo but you can also use cooked squid or chicken. If using chicken, choose a small fillet (a thigh or half a breast is just the right size) and shred the cooked meat.

Ingredients

For the Dressing:

1 teaspoon fish sauce

1 tablespoon lime juice (or lemon or kalamansi)

1 bird's eye chili (finely sliced)

1/8 teaspoon ginger (grated)

1/8 teaspoon garlic (minced)

1 teaspoon sugar

For the Salad:

3 to 4 medium-sized shrimps

Salt to taste

Pepper to taste

1/2 cup pomelo pulp (shredded)

1/2 cup fresh mung bean sprouts (rinsed and drained well)

6 to 8 lemon basil leaves

6 to 8 mint leaves

3 sprigs of cilantro

Steps to Make It

1. Make the dressing. In a small jar with a screw-type cap, pour in the fish sauce and lime juice. Add the sliced chili, grated ginger, minced garlic, and sugar. Pour in two tablespoonfuls of water. Screw on the cap and shake until the sugar is dissolved. Set aside to allow the flavors to develop while you prepare the rest of the ingredients for the salad.
2. Cut off the heads of the shrimps. Peel off the shells but leave the tails on. Make a shallow cut along the back of each shrimp and pull off the black thread inside (it's the shrimp's digestive system and you do not want to eat it). Toss the shrimps with a little salt and pepper. Cook by steaming, broiling or grilling. Do not overcook.
3. In a mixing bowl, put the shredded pomelo, mung bean sprouts, basil, mint, and cilantro. Toss lightly using your hands.
4. Scoop out the pomelo mixture and arrange on a salad plate. Arrange the shrimps on top. Sprinkle in the nuts. Drizzle the prepared dressing over the salad.

Pandan Rice and Mung Bean Cake Recipe

Rice is to Asia what wheat is to most of the Western world. And while the West has vanilla for its go-to flavoring, in Asia, there is pandan. Traditional cakes, many flavored with pandan, are made with rice flour. And because ovens, as they are known in the West, are not native to Asia, rice cakes are often steamed rather than baked.

If you can find split mung beans, use them as they cook much faster than whole mung beans.

While nothing compares to fresh coconut milk, if you have difficulty making it from freshly grated coconut, use canned coconut milk or coconut powder dispersed in warm water.

Ingredients

For the Yellow Layer:

1/2 cup split yellow mung beans

1/2 cup tapioca starch

1/4 cup rice flour (not glutinous)

2/3 to 3/4 cup sugar

1 pinch salt

1/2 cup coconut milk

For the Green Layer:

1 1/4 cups tapioca starch

1/2 cup rice flour

2/3 to 3/4 cup sugar

1 pinch salt

2 cups pandan water

Steps to Make It

Rinse the mung beans several times. Place in a bowl and pour in two cups of water. Discard any piece that floats to the surface. Cover loosely and leave to soak for at least four hours. Overnight in the refrigerator is recommended.

Rinse the beans several times again. Drain and pour into a pan. Pour in about a cup and a half of water.

Bring to the boil. Cover, lower the heat and simmer until mushy. Depending on the quality of the beans, this can take anywhere from half an hour to an hour and a half. Add water, a quarter cup at a time, if the mixture dries up before the beans are soft. Turn off the heat cool completely.

When the cooked beans have cooled, strain to remove any excess water. Pour the beans into the blender Add the sugar and salt and puree. Stir together the coconut milk, rice flour, and tapioca starch. Add to the beans and process until smooth.

Stir together all the ingredients for the green layer.

Prepare the steamer. Pour water into the pan and start heating it to boiling point.

Lightly spray eight to 12 single-serve ramekins.

Pour about two tablespoonfuls of the green mixture into each ramekin. Arrange the ramekins in the steamer basket and steam for about seven minutes or until the top of the green layer is firm to the touch.

Divide the yellow mixture among the ramekins. Steam for 10 to 12 minutes or until firm.

Divide the remaining green mixture among the ramekins. Steam for another five to seven minutes.

Loosen the cakes with an oiled knife. Serve warm or at room temperature. You may drizzle them with more coconut milk and sprinkle with toasted sesame seeds.

Pork Bone and Green Papaya Soup

In Asia, no part of the pig goes to waste. In cooking Vietnamese green papaya soup, the pig's feet are traditionally used. Although they contain little to no meat, they are rich in tendons which liquefy and become part of the broth during the long and slow cooking.

Although papaya is a fruit, unripe green papaya is cooked as a vegetable in Southeast Asia. The flesh, after cooking, is soft but firm and has a foamy texture. It is bland, almost tasteless, but able to soak up the flavors of ingredients it is cooked with.

How to Cook

It takes several hours to cook pig's feet to get it to that stage when the flesh separates from the bone and much of the tendon has liquefied into the broth. If you're going to simmer the pig's feet on the stovetop, use a pot with a thick bottom to minimize the chance of the pork feet sticking to the bottom and scorching.

A pressure cooker may be used and it might be the most convenient method. Although pressure cooking will cook the pig's feet faster, it does not make a thorough job of drawing out the flavors from the bones.

We find the slow cooker to be the ideal equipment for cooking tough cuts of meat like pork feet. No stirring is necessary and the broth tastes like every bit of flavor have been squeezed off the bones.

Ingredients

2.2 pounds/1 kilo pig's feet

2 cloves garlic

2 slices ginger

1 shallot (unpeeled and cut into halves)

Fish sauce (to taste)

Sugar (to taste)

1 green papaya

Steps to Make It

Gather the ingredients.

Rinse the pig's feet. Scrub thoroughly. Rinse once more. If there are visible hairs, use a kitchen torch to burn them off. Chop the pig's feet into serving size pieces.

Place the prepared pig's feet in a pan. Cover with water. Boil for ten minutes. Drain and rinse the pig's feet thoroughly.

Transfer the pig's feet to the slow cooker. Add the garlic, ginger, and shallot. Drizzle in about two tablespoonfuls of fish sauce. Add a teaspoonful of sugar. Pour in enough water to cover the pig's feet and make a substantial amount of broth. (Leave enough space as you will be adding the green papaya later.)

Set the slow cooker to high. After two hours set the heat to low and continue cooking the pig's feet for another five hours.

Cut the green papaya lengthwise into halves. Using a spoon, scoop out the seeds and fibrous center of the papaya.

Use a vegetable peeler to remove the skin. Cut the flesh into two-inch cubes.

Taste the broth. Add more fish sauce and sugar, as needed.

Add the green papaya to the slow cooker. If there is room, stir. Replace the cover and cook for another hour.

Taste the broth one last time. Adjust the seasonings once more, if needed.

Stir in the scallions and serve the soup.

Enjoy!

Noodle Salad With Lemongrass Beef (Bun bo xao)

Bún bò xào is a noodle salad, but in Southeast Asia, bún bò xào would be considered a light meal rather than a starter course as a salad is often defined in the West. Bún bò xào has everything that a balanced meal requires. It has meat, it has carbohydrates it has lots of vegetables and fresh herbs.

Bún bò xào is served in layers. At the bottom of the bowl are the cooked rice noodles (bún) cooled to room temperature. The noodles are topped with vegetables, both pickled and fresh. Next comes the beef (bò) that had been marinated with lemongrass then stir-fried (xào). The garnishes come last. Crushed roasted peanuts, fried crisp shallots and lots of fresh herbs that may include cilantro, lemon basil,

51

mint, perilla (shisho leaves) or all of them. A generous splash of nuoc mam pha (more popularly known as nuoc cham, the generic term for dipping sauce) is added, the contents of the bowl are tossed together and the bún bò xào is ready to be enjoyed.

Bún bò xào is comforting and familiar yet nuanced enough to be mysterious at the same time. It's all about the contrasting hues and textures of the ingredients which are happily brought together by nước mắm pha without which the salad is nothing but a discordant lump of colors and shapes.

Ingredients

8 ounces (about 250 grams) beef sirloin

1 tablespoon nước mắm (fish sauce)

1 teaspoon garlic (minced)

1 tablespoon finely sliced lemongrass (use only the tender center of the white portion of the stalks)

4 ounces (110 grams) thin rice noodles, (prepared according to package directions then drained and cooled)

1/3 cup julienned cucumber

1/3 cup pickled carrot and radish

1 finger chili, thinly sliced (optional)

1 tablespoon peanut oil

2 cups fresh herbs (cilantro, lemon basil, mint, perilla or a combination of two or more)

1 tablespoon crushed roasted peanuts

2 tablespoons fried crisp shallots (available in Asian stores)

1/3 cup nước mắm

Steps to Make It

Cut the sirloin across the grain into slices less than a quarter of an inch thick. Cut each slice into strips about half an inch wide. Mix with the nước mắm (fish sauce), garlic and lemongrass.

Divide the noodles between two bowls. Top with the julienned cucumber, pickled carrot and radish and finger chili (if using).

Heat the peanut oil in a wok to smoking point. Stir-fry the beef for about two minutes.

Divide the beef between the two bowls.

Top with fresh herbs, peanuts, and fried shallots.

Serve with nước mắm pha on the side.

Pickled Bitter Melon/Gourd Salad

Thin slices of bitter melon (bitter gourd) are combined with julienned radish and carrot to make a refreshingly delicious pickled salad that can be served as a side dish to meat and seafood dishes.

The recipes for two dressings are given below, one with Filipino flavors and the other with Vietnamese flavors. This is a meatless dish but note that the Vietnamese dressing contains fish sauce. For a totally vegan salad, use salt in place of the fish sauce.

Ingredients

1 cup bitter melon (thinly sliced)

1/4 cup radish (julienned)

1/4 cup carrot (julienned)

1 shallot (thinly sliced)

2 - 3 bird's eye chilies (thinly sliced)

Steps to Make It

Place all the ingredients in a bowl. Toss well. Transfer to a jar with a screw-type cap.

Choose and make one of the following pickling solutions.

Filipino-style:

1 cup white vinegar

1/2 to 3/4 cup white sugar

1 teaspoon salt

1 clove of garlic (crushed)

2 slices of ginger

1/2 teaspoon freshly ground black pepper

Boil all the ingredients together until the sugar is completely dissolved. Cool.

Vietnamese-style:

1 cup lime juice

1/2 to 3/4 cup white sugar

2 tablespoons fish sauce (use 1 tablespoon salt for a vegan version)

2 cloves garlic (crushed)

2 slices of ginger

Place all the ingredients in a jar with a screw-type cap. Shake until the sugar is completely dissolved.

When you have made your pickling solution, pour it into the jar containing the vegetables. Allow to steep overnight. The vegetables taste even better when allowed to steep longer.

The pickled bitter melon salad is delicious as it is but there are a few ingredients to make it even better:

Top the salad with fresh herbs for brighter flavors. Finely snipped scallions, torn basil, mint, and cilantro are all good.

Garnish the pickled bitter melon salad with crisp fried shallots or toasted garlic bits, or both! Not only will they add boldness to the flavors, but the slight crunch also provides an interesting contrast as well.

Sprinkle toasted nuts over the salad. Cashew nuts or peanuts work especially well. Just chop the nuts, throw into a medium-hot oil-free pan and toast until the nuts glisten with their oil. Cool before adding to the salad.

Use toasted sesame seeds instead of nuts or combine sesame seeds with nuts. Toast the sesame seeds the same way you would the nuts.

Want to turn the bitter melon salad into a main dish? Throw in some poached or grilled chicken fillets or shrimps and you're good to go.

The pickled bitter melon will keep in the fridge for several days. For best results, every time you take out a portion for a meal, make sure that the remaining vegetables are still submerged in the pickling solution.

Wrapping Vietnamese Spring Rolls for Frying

Cha Gio, Vietnamese spring rolls, are eaten either fresh and uncooked or fried. Before doing either they need to be folded and rolled in a particular way. Wrapping up a spring roll may look difficult, but it is really quite easy once you get the hang of it. After wrapping a few, you will start to feel like an expert.

Before you start, you will need to make the filling for the Vietnamese Spring Roll:

1 small head cabbage (shredded and cooked)

2 ounces shiitakes (thinly sliced and cooked)

2 cooked diced shallots

1/2 pound ground pork

1/2 pound shrimp (minced)

You also need 24 dry rice paper wrappers (6.3-inch/16cm or 8.7-inch/22cm diameter) and a bowl or rimmed plate of water.

Set up for Soaking and Filling the Rice Paper Wrappers

Set up your filling, water, and rice wrappers. The dried rice paper wrapper needs to be softened before wrapping. To do this, fill a shallow bowl with some tap or filtered water (some people add a tablespoon or so of sugar or mix the water with rice wine to help the wrappers brown when they're fried).

Take one rice paper wrapper and immerse it completely in the water. Make sure that the wrapper is completely wet. Wait about 30 seconds for the wrapper to soften. It will turn malleable and start to stick to the plate but that's ok.

Note: If you use warm water, the paper will soften considerably faster. However, this may not work in your favor if you are new at it.

Fill the Moistened Rice Wrapper

Put the wet wrapper on a large empty plate or cutting board. Place 1 heaping tablespoon of the filling about 1 inch from the edge of the wrapper, on the side closest to you. Using the back of a spoon, press the filling flat into the shape of a small chocolate bar.

Folding the Wrapper Forward

Begin the folding process. First, fold the edge of the wrapper closest to you so that it covers the filling. Make sure that this first fold completely covers the filling, and pull the edge of the fold slightly under the filling making a taut, small parcel.

Folding the Sides

Next, fold one side. Using both your hands, fold the right side of the wrapper toward the center, stopping where the filling is. Do the same with the other side—fold the left side of the wrapper toward the center, stopping where the filling is.

Keep Folding Forward

Continue folding the wrapper by grabbing the enclosed filling and turning it over until it reaches the end of the wrapper. Check all sides to make sure there are no loose ends on the wrapper. This ensures the filling won't escape when frying.

Ready to be Fried

Now your Vietnamese spring roll is ready to be fried.

If you're not going to fry the spring rolls right away, line them all up on a plate and cover with plastic wrap so that they do not dry up. Make sure that the spring rolls do not touch each other, as they can be a bit sticky and may tear if you need to pull them apart. Alternatively, you may freeze the wrapped spring rolls to be cooked at another time.

If there is any leftover filling, you can always freeze it for another Vietnamese spring roll occasion.

Fry Away

You can fully deep fry the rolls if you have a deep fryer and/or enough oil. It is also possible to "shallow fry" the rolls by filling a pot with about 1 inch of peanut, canola, or other frying oil. Heat the oil over medium-high heat until the oil measures about 350 F, reduce the heat to low-medium to maintain the temperature. Add only as many rolls as will fit in a single layer without touching. Fry on each side until blistered and browned. Drain on a cooling rack set over a baking sheet or on layers of paper towels. Repeat in batches until all rolls are fried.

Serve with fresh lettuce, mint, cilantro, and basil, as well as nuoc cham dipping sauce.

Printed in Dunstable, United Kingdom

65945760R00037